Rags 2 Riches: Lessons from the Hard Road

By

Manuel Simpson

Prologue

Manuel Simpson's odyssey starts in the rich although barren soil of the Delta region of Indianola, Mississippi and the southwest section of Tunica County, whose rhythm of lives was set by the earth and Matt family ties. He was one of six children and given birth in a world that was filled with sacrifice, hard work and constant fight for existence. His parents named Hattie and Robert stayed strong and knew how to respect the community and the life as well as taught their children. Manuel's childhood was set on the beats of cotton paddies; his young body moved with sacks of cotton, and his hands wore the roughness of the adolescent who toiled under the burning Mississippian sky. Education at Carver Elementary was not the priority at that point, as was the struggle for the family's existence, and Manuel was trying to balance between attending school and working as a child in a factory. But even in such a harsh environment a small flicker of resistance started germinating inside of him. The following year, in 1967, the family relocated to Maywood; a complete contrast to the vast fields of Mississippi. The streets crowded and massive constructions were an unfamiliar environment for a boy who grew up in the country. Here Manuel gets new challenges of living in urban society. He is entrusted with responsibilities more than his age can handle. However, there was hope and with it clutched tightly to the boy, Manuel. He looked past the bars of poverty and of restriction, the boy decided with his own free will that he wanted to make his own destiny. Graduation marked a crossroads with a stable production line job with the hope of a college education. Manuel did the latter and headed on a journey to redefine his future the way he wanted it. This Autobiography covers the success story of Manuel, a man who could overcome addiction and had to face prison, and severed relationships. Even through, all this hope continued to be his beacon of light—a rather strong indication of his optimism that at some point in the middle of all, change is always possible.

Acknowledgment

It is for this reason that this story would not come into existence, if not for the support, inspiration and many lessons I have learned along the way. I hold special appreciation to my parents Hattie and Robert for having laid great emphasis on working hard, perseverance and togetherness in the family. The things they did in the cotton fields of Indianola, Mississippi are the things which I have learnt are value of hard work no matter how tough things are. To the people who were around me in those early years of my life, thank you for demonstrating to me the power that is in 'the collective' and 'trials'. Living in Maywood, Illinois had its own share of challenges and discoveries, to the people who motivated me to overcome the odds. Every conversation and event in my life led me to this discovery of self and kept me motivated to create a better future. I also want to express my deep appreciation to my children who raised the bar of accountability, forgiveness and love within me. Their existence in my life as the reality I got back was giving me a new meaning in life. I am very grateful to my project manager, Kavin Jones who assist me in each and every step in completing the book. Lastly, this story is for all those who have rightly suffered, struggled to get their freedom back and dream again. May it encourage everyone to accept their path and get comfort in the possibility a power of belief holds.

I am also grateful to Mr. Kevin Jones from Ebook Writing Experts in assisting me to write and published this book and let my dream come true to write this book.

Dedication

This book is dedicated to all the people who influenced my life and the incredible story I am fortunate to share. To all those who have believed in me, let alone when I faced serious challenges, I am grateful. In my young age, the word 'help' has been shaped by my father who bust his life in order to provide shelter for the family, my teachers, relatives, friends and everyone who encouraged me. This is dedicated to those whose life narratives are intertwined with mine. My strength has been a testament of God's Grace to me. So, to any of you who have gone through addiction, tough times, or the even the rough times in life, know that my victory over addiction, my fight against personal demons, and my opposition against obstacles are yours. You are not alone. This book is also dedicated to the divine favor, direction, and blessings that I have experienced in my entire life. This can only be by the divine purpose and plan to use me to be a blessing to people as I have matured through each chapter of my book.

Table of Contents

Introduction

Life often takes us through a journey of twists and turns, achievements and failures, joys and heartaches. As I share my story, it is not just my voice that resonates but the voices of many who have walked similar paths those who have struggled, stumbled, and found the strength to rise again. Born in the fields of Mississippi and shaped by the unyielding hands of hardship, my life has been a testament to resilience and redemption. From enduring the harsh realities of segregation and laboring under the blistering southern sun to confronting personal demons of addiction, incarceration, and fractured relationships, I stand as proof that the human spirit can overcome the most daunting adversities.

This autobiography is not just my story; it is a beacon of hope for anyone who has faced moments of despair, for those who have wondered if there is a way out of the darkness. It is a story of second chances and the transformative power of determination, education, and belief in oneself. As you turn the pages of this book, I invite you to walk with me through the fields of Indianola, the bustling streets of Maywood, and the deeply personal battles that defined my journey. Together, let us explore the lessons learned and the achievements achieved not as an end but as a continual process of growth and faith. This is my story, but it is also yours, for within each of us lies the power to forge a better tomorrow.

Chapter 1: Roots in the South

The life story of Manuel Simpson begins in Indianola, Mississippi, with the cadence of life ruled by the land and a binding force of family. He was one of six children born into a family that knew dimes, nickels, sacrifice, and hard work. From his young years, he learned respect for everything around him, nurtured by a community that values endurance and resilience. His mother, Hattie, and his father, Robert, anchored his family, and they lived very close to the earth-off its bounty-like so many families in rural Southern communities. Yet, even here, every day was a battle against greater forces than themselves: poverty, prejudice, mere survival.

By 1967, Manuel's world was work and responsibilities-he would rise well before the sun crept over the horizon, air cool and heavy, promising yet another scorching day in the cotton fields. His school was Carver Elementary, but more often than not, concerns that took precedence over education were grossly immediate needs of the family. There wasn't an issue of school or work; there was a balancing act between the two. Outside of the classroom, one could have found Manuel in the field, a burlap sack slung over his small shoulders, picking cotton under the unrelenting Mississippi sun. There was no such thing as weekends, no such thing as an extended summer vacation; just work from sunup to sundown, hands raw and callous from grasping the thorny stems.

Even at sundown, when today's fieldwork was done, his work at home remained. The small homestead of his family depended on all members' help. In the backyard, chickens clucked; Manuel would dart out to feed them before they became restless. Eggs had to be gathered in, often hidden in some dark nook underneath the house so that Manuel needed to crawl through dirt and cobwebs, feeling in the dark, blindly. There were rows of crops his father had planted painfully and demanded the work of watering and weeding; besides, there

11

always seemed to be plenty of wood which must be chopped down or water to be hauled up from the old well.

Life was hard in Mississippi, and the cultural landscape around him was no less unforgiving. Manuel's time and place nestled segregation firmly in his grasps when opportunities were few and survival the only option. His family, like most others, lived in a house set upon cinder blocks with thin walls that did little to ward off the biting winter cold or the sweltering summer heat. It was here, however, that Manuel learned some of his most valuable lessons: the value of hard work, the importance of family, and the code of dignity-an unspoken one, to be sure-that his parents had held on to, even in the face of adverse circumstances.

Sundays provided the one respite from the week's backbreaking labor. The Simpsons would don their finest-clothing washed and scrubbed by hand in a foot tub, hung out to dry on a clothesline strung between two sagging fence posts. Church had been a solemn ritual, a place where Manuel and his siblings would sit in a pew made of hard wood, the smell of starch and soap still clinging to their crisply ironed shirts. They would sing hymns and listen to sermons of hope and redemption-words that almost seemed to be from a foreign world, as their worth was measured in pounds of cotton that could be picked or the hours which could be labored.

Rags 2 Riches: Lessons from the Hard Road

Where Sundays were a time to worship for them, it was the shortest breathing times for Manuel from the drudgery of his daily routine. He would watch other children in the congregation, bright-eyed with dreams about what lay beyond the cotton fields. But to him, dreams were things he just couldn't afford. Days bled into days of more chores: house cleaning, babysitting the younger siblings, and tending to the hogs. What little free time he had was invested in helping his father fix up the place, practicing his carpentry skills in the hope that someday they would amount to something bigger.

It wasn't just the physical labor that shaped him, but the emotional and mental strength of always being at a disadvantage. Life in Indianola taught him how to persevere against stacked odds, how to be resilient towards one's own success. Very few avenues came forward to better one's fortunes, and the family's future was as fragile as the crops they tended. Still, amidst this hardship, Manuel's parents imbued in him a silent pride and a fierce resolve to forge ahead.

Years just blended together in a blur of sweat and labor, flashes of instants of happiness. Manuel's family farmed the land as if trying to carve out a chunk of the world that was denied to them. Still, the feeling that they struggled against something immovable was always there. Their house told that struggle-what a small, simple house stood standing as a living ridiculed symbol of the family's resilience and its limitations. There was no running water; the family drew all its water for cooking and drinking from a well and bathed in a washbasin under the sky.

That was the only life Manuel knew, and he was genuinely too afraid of being taken out of that life. Still, he felt ready-to be free from the endless circle of work, the monotony of the fields, and the suffocating heat that seemed to smother every hope and ambition. So, in 1969, the family packed what little they had and boarded a Greyhound bus bound for a new life up North.

Manuel had no idea what to expect in Illinois, but really, he could have imagined nothing more different from the world he knew. The bus cut its way up through new landscapes, and he gawked at the view out the window. He had never seen skyscrapers before, never stood at a street corner where automobiles whizzed by in a blur of motion that was constant. Everything was larger than life: the buildings towering above him, people rushing past each other as if they were caught up in some grand pursuit that he couldn't quite understand.

Getting off that bus was something like entering a different world. Compared to those unpaved roads in Indianola, the streets of Illinois were a far cry, and to a boy who was used to getting down dirt paths lined with crops, the city was terrifyingly exciting. However, Manuel knew one thing: he'd have to learn this place, make it his own. It wouldn't be easy, but if there was one thing life in Mississippi had taught him, it was how to adapt and survive.

The cotton fields and the long days of labor were now behind him, but the lessons they had taught him would remain forever.

Chapter 2: The Big Move – Heading North

The point of permanently relocating outside the South marked a turning point for the Simpson family-to be spared from the infinite drudgery of struggle and hard work that defined the lives of these people in Mississippi. For years, unending farm work, livestock rearing, making ends meet on a small house built over cinder blocks had been a struggle. But this promise of a new start in the North seemed a dream-so far away until finally within grasp. When Manuel's father announced, they were heading to Illinois, there was no turning back. It was

1969, and, carrying little more than their clothes, their hope that life up North would be different-easier, maybe, or at least full of opportunity-the family boarded a Greyhound bus.

His stomach churned with excitement and fear. To leave Indianola was to leave behind everything he knew: friends, neighbors, the order of daily life. Yet, the opportunity to behold something new beyond the dusty roads and endless cotton fields stirred something in him. As the bus rumbled down highways and through small towns, he still wondered what the North would be like. He had been told of edifices that apparently scraped the sky, cities teeming with people in finery, driving sleek cars. The stories told only part of the truth. Nothing could have prepared Manuel for the culture shock awaiting him in Maywood, Illinois.

Getting off the bus into Maywood, Illinois was like entering another world. Considering the size, Maywood Illinois wasn't a sprawling metropolis, but to a boy who grew up in a town where the next field over stretched to the horizon, it was close enough to New York City to overwhelm him. So many people. They walked with a purpose and urgency in the steps and their expressions fixed. Everything was huge, noisier, and somehow more extreme. The streets were lined with tall buildings that loomed above him, casting long shadows that made Manuel feel small and out of place. He gasped in wonder at the sight of automobiles whizzing by in a ceaseless blur of motion, their horns blaring some sort of chaotic symphony that seemed to echo off the brick and steel around him.

Beneath all that novelty and excitement lay the hard reality of a new beginning. Maywood Illinois was a city of contrasts-prosperous in some quarters, rundown in others, racially divided in ways that Manuel might hardly have imagined. If the North was some kind of Promised Land, offering opportunities at every turn, it didn't take long to figure out the Simpsons' would be hard. The first issue that had to be resolved was the matter of where to live. Housing was high, and housing opportunities open to Black families were scarce. Days of searching ended with their settling into a small, cramped apartment on the west side of town, far from the modest but familiar home they had lived in.

Establishing life in the North tried the patience of every single family member, but Manuel struggled most. School was supposed to be his refuge, a place where he could first focus and study for a brighter future. But that hope quickly faded when he realized just how different things were in Maywood Illinois. His first day at Emerson School was a blur of strange faces and unfamiliar routines. He often found himself standing out for reasons that made him most uncomfortable. Whereas, the school in Indianola had been much smaller, its classrooms filled with kids he had known his whole life, at Emerson he was just another new face-a curiosity to some, an outsider to most.

The curriculum was more advanced, the teachers more demanding, and the expectations far higher than what he was used to. Though Manuel had always been a good student, he struggled to keep up with his classmates, many of whom had been raised in an environment where education was prioritized and resources were ample. But even more discouraging was knowing day in and day out that while he was in school, his family was counting on him to bring in a contribution. He felt the burden at home was enormous, which seemed to grow with each night as he stepped into their small apartment, seeing it in the lines of his parents' faces.

It seemed as if it would be impossible to balance work with school. His father managed to find work at a local factory, often working long hours just to make ends meet. His mother began cleaning, her hands raw and chafed from scrubbing the floors of homes for people who often looked directly through her as if she didn't exist. Manuel, not quite a teenager yet, started seeking ways in which he might earn an after-school income. He took any odd job he could find: delivering newspapers, running errands for neighbors, working in the backrooms of local stores sorting through stock, and cleaning up.

The physical strain was one thing, the emotional toll quite another. Every time he dressed in his work clothes and headed out to earn some dollars, he couldn't help but feel that he lagged further and further behind. Watching other kids his age stroll along home from school, laughing together with the biggest worry something like whether they'd make the basketball team or pass some tough math test, he couldn't help but think of himself as falling further behind. For Manuel, life was much more involved. He still valued education, but in this juncture of his life, survival was first-and that meant setting aside his dreams for the time being and pushing through exhaustion day after day.

The early years in Maywood Illinois were defined by the struggle between continuing his education and helping his family survive. He struggled to keep up at Emerson School, staying after class, asking the teachers questions in hopes of bridging the gap between himself and the kids whose parents had other means. Yet even as he pushed himself, the need to work hung over him like a shadow. It was always tug of war, one he was afraid he could never win.

It would not be long before Manuel realized the promise of a better life up North came with its own set of challenges.

Rags 2 Riches: Lessons from the Hard Road

While, Maywood Illinois might have had more opportunities on paper, those opportunities were not equally available to everyone. A new kind of prejudice, subtle in ways that the Mississippi kind had not been, but no less painful met him. There were whole neighborhoods he wasn't welcome in, certain stores whose clerks followed him too closely-as if he'd steal-some classrooms where teachers treated him as less able, less worthy.

But even with all these, Manuel had never weakened his resolve. He knew he just could not give in now since his parents had sacrificed enough to bring the family this far. He kept pushing and kept fighting, determined that he was going to show that he belonged and could rise above what was expected of him. He'd wake up every morning before dawn, struggle through his schoolwork, run to whatever job he could find and then come home long after the darkness fell, exhausted but refusing to give up.

The move to Maywood Illinois was much more than a geographic shift; it was a test in fire that would mold Manuel into what he was going to become. He knew it wouldn't be easy; the road to success would indeed be paved with hard work, but with perseverance in the face of doubt and discrimination. It did not come easy, and sometimes there were days Manuel wondered if they made the right decision by leaving Mississippi. But each day in Maywood Illinois-to each small victory, every hard-earned dollar- he took one step closer to building the life his parents had dreamed of, a life that would take their family from rags to riches in a single generation.

Chapter 3: Navigating the Challenges of Adolescence

As Manuel Simpson entered his early teens, those stresses from trying to balance work with school increased, as did those of adolescence brought on by internal and external factors. Living in Maywood Illinois, certainly was not the dream he had in mind when he first left Mississippi. Now living in the North proved to be just as demanding, if not more so. Piling on the stress of living in a segregated, racially divided city, attempting to keep up academically, and helping out his family financially made for an emotional burden hard to handle.

When in Emerson School, Manuel was an exception among the rest because he was new there and more importantly, he came from South, and everything around was different and required his adaptation in one way or another to Northern pattern of life. The academic course load was more challenging, and he felt it difficult to keep pace with peers who had grown up under better conditions of socialization and education. Teachers seemed more impatient, and some students were not welcoming but viewed him as an outsider. These growing feelings of alienation finally started seeping into his self-confidence, yet Manuel refused to give in to discouragement. He started staying after school on a regular basis, asking questions-many times attempting to review material he had not grasped in class. Even with these measures, he still felt he was playing catch-up.

Socially, Manuel had difficulties mixing with children of his age. While others would kill time after school or play sports, Manuel was doing lots of odd jobs and running errands to keep his family alive. However small, other kids of his age could afford to invest some serious mind energy into teenage concerns: girls, athletic teams, and Friday night football games. Manuel envied kids who walked casually home, their shoulders off from responsibilities. Whatever the hardships were, Manuel was resistant, believing that one day all his efforts would pay off.

At home, the weight of responsibility mounted with each passing day. His father toiled for long hours at a factory, while his mother cleaned houses, arriving home day in and day out with swollen hands and raw skin from scrubbing floors. As the eldest child, Manuel felt the pressure that he, too, was expected to do his share. Odd jobs after school drove him to work, as would anyone else in his place, with seriousness to help see food on the table. The management of all these with homework and responsibilities required at home brought an overwhelming sense at times; however, lessons of perseverance learnt in Mississippi were still steadfast in his character. He knew he had to push through even when the load seemed insurmountable.

At an emotional level, Manuel went through a very turbulent period in adolescence. He longed for the freedom and carefree life of his peers on one hand, while on the other hand, he knew the sacrifices his parents had made just to make life better for him. While other kids of his age complained about curfew or homework, Manuel worried about whether his family would have food on the table, or how they would pay the rent and survive in their apartment on the west side of

Maywood Illinois. The move North had promised opportunity, but it came with its own struggles. Segregation and prejudice reared their heads in Maywood Illinois, even if less overt than in Mississippi.

Manuel also dealt with a different kind of racism, be it following him around stores or low expectations in school.

And yet, amidst all that, Manuel's resolve hardened; he felt that if he kept pushing on, a stop could be put to the hardships that had hitherto characterized generations of life back in his family.

Books became his solace, and he borrowed extensively from the local library to add to his knowledge and relieve the monotony of his everyday existence. Thus, reading became a passion, and through reading, he learned about leaders and figures who have surmounted extraordinary odds. Stories of triumph became sources of inspiration to him. He knew that if he ever tried to do better for a future, for himself and his family, he had to keep his eyes on the prize and never be defeated by temporary setbacks. However, with adolescence came both challenges and the germination of Manuel's self-awareness, the beginning of asking himself what kind of life he wanted to live.

Everything that happened to him in Maywood Illinois changed his interpretation of the world and his place in it.

Manuel vowed not to become like all those around him who had fallen into a trap. He saw how one could easily lose hope, with the heavy burden of expectations tugging at them from one side and limitations from the other-economic limitations. Yet, he refused to give in to despair.

Hard work, perseverance instilled by his parents, and a deep sense of responsibility are what kept him surefooted through this period. The struggles of the family were his own; every obstacle faced was one more reason for Manuel to be successful. Slowly but surely, Manuel was building that mental toughness which would serve him so well in the years to come.

Chapter 4: A Fork in the Road – Choosing a Path

As Manuel's high school graduation neared, he became increasingly motivated. The end of his school years meant a fork in the road when he would have to make a choice about his future. Most of his life he had been spending his days in a maddening effort of survival and building up his family. Now, for the first time in his life, he was forced to really think about what he wanted to do for himself. The only problem was that both immediate and long-term futures were looking equally uncertain.

Graduation was an accomplishment that many in his family had ever achieved. His parents, both products of the Deep South, had received minimal educations due to the economic pressures of their youth. In that sense, education was an important unreachable thing for them. Gradually receiving his diploma at the stage was Manuel's personal merit but symbolic to his entire family-to break the chains of poverty and limitation that followed them from Mississippi up to Illinois. But as the euphoria washed off, reality set in: *What now?*

His father expected him to find work, as he had done when he left school. The financial needs of the family were unquestionably pressing, and Manuel felt the weight of responsibility weighing on him more than ever. The factory where his father labored was always hiring on young men who were willing to put in long hours for regular pay. It was a good position for him to follow-most of his friends were already working there and earning good salaries, therefore helping their families. At the same time, Manuel always dreamed of something bigger. He never wanted to waste his life on some factory floor, exchanging his youth for a check that would only keep the family afloat. Education opened Manuel's eyes to a world of possibilities other than those narrowly confined within his immediate circumstances.

He did alright in certain subject areas, especially the math and science courses, and his teachers had put the idea of college in his mind. This intrigued him but at the same time intimidated him. None of his family members had ever been to college. Leaving home, given the financial and emotional dependence of his parents and siblings upon him, had been almost unthinkable. Yet in his heart of hearts, Manuel knew that unless he seized this opportunity, he might never get another one to break himself free from the cycles of poverty and hardship that had so far characterized his life.

Graduation loomed, with his inner conflict marked correspondingly.

He felt the obligation to stay as close to home as possible and help the family, doing his part to keep them alive, yet on the other hand, he realized unless he made the leap, he might well get stuck in that kind of struggle all of his life. It was a prospect he so dreaded from his life-being stuck in factory work for decades and never pushing his full potential.

One afternoon, a guidance counsellor took him to one side, having noticed that this was a problem. He was an older man, gentle in his manner; he had seen a lot of boys like Manuel, kids smart and willing who were nonetheless kept back by circumstances.

He sat Manuel down and asked him to take a minute to consider what he truly wanted out of a future. *"You're a special kid, Manuel," he said.* "I see it in the way you work, I see it in your commitment. You don't have to decide now, but don't be afraid to dream bigger. You can go to college. There are scholarships out there. You just have to be willing to look.". That stuck with Manuel, as it was the first time that anyone outside his family believed he had the capability for doing something greater. The idea of college had always just been this really vague and afar concept, but now, for the first time, it felt attainable. Over the following weeks, Manuel began researching colleges and scholarships. He would spend hours in the library, reading about available financial aid options and programs that could help students from low-income backgrounds. The more he read, the more resolute he became.

Yet, it was still far from an easy decision to make. Manuel was wracked with guilt at the thought of leaving his family behind, knowing full well how crucial his contribution was to household income. But his parents had pride in his supposed work at school, yet remained wholly skeptical about the whole idea of college: they couldn't understand how it could be helpful to him in some day when he manned up, and they would miss his contribution too much. Yet, Manuel knew that pursuing higher education was his only real chance to escape not only the limitations of his upbringing but also to create a better future for himself and his family.

As graduation day came and went, Manuel found himself at a crossroads. The job at the factory was waiting, and the paycheck that would come from it could immediately alleviate his family's financial struggles. But the pull of college-the idea of expanding his horizons of achieving something beyond what he had ever imagined-was too great to turn down. In the end, this was a question that forced Manuel to decide one way or another, to set his life in one direction or another. He then applied to colleges and took steps to secure financial aid. The decision wasn't easy, but it was right for him. He decided to take control of his destiny, however dark the road ahead may seem.

Chapter 5: The College Years – Expanding Horizons

When Manuel went to college, it was one of those new phases in life- filled with both excitement and trepidation. This was the first time in his life that Manuel had to leave his home-a thing very daunting in nature. While his family had been the center of his world for most parts of his life, now he was stepping into the unknown. Living on campus with students from highly variable backgrounds intimidated him. But with the fear was the determination to make this opportunity count.

He had worked much too hard to allow self-doubt to stand in the way.

The first weeks of college were overwhelming, and Manuel realized, more or less quickly, that he was not as academically prepared as many of his classmates.

While other students seemed to pass through assignments and exams with flying colors, Manuel always struggled to keep up. There was a huge gap between his high school education and what was expected at college level, but he did not give up. Manuel spent several hours in the library studying his textbooks and notes. And as days passed, all his effort started to pay off little by little. Socially, college for Manuel was another whole world.

He grew up in a close community of people knowing each other; now he was thrown into the lion's den of sorts, where Manuel became just one of several thousand students. It would be a little time, but he slowly started making friends. Many of these friendships came through similar experiences: students who came from backgrounds similar to his and who also faced struggles of being first-generation college students. It is a connection that brings some sense of comradeship and support that Manuel did not expect to find.

As the months passed, Manuel began to take up new interests and passions. One of the professors recognized that he was particularly good in math and suggested that he ought to try majoring in engineering. At first, Manuel felt intimidated: Engineering sounded like a degree for kids who came from richer families, kids who had gone to better high schools and who'd had higher levels of training. The more he thought about this, though, the more he knew this was just what he needed. Manuel had struggled all his life, and to enter a field that required great mental effort, with high pay, seemed very luring.

Convinced by his professors and friends, Manuel decided to major in electrical engineering. The classes were difficult, and many times he felt that perhaps he had not made the right decision of area of study. But whenever it did-every time the doubt seeped in-he thought about how far he'd already climbed, about his family's sacrifices to bring him here, about the struggles he'd had in Maywood Illinois, and how much grit it took to survive high school.

College also provided Manuel with personal growth that went beyond academics. He joined every student organization that would have him, including a mentorship program for disadvantaged high school students. This is how Manuel could return to his community for the opportunity he received by means of sharing his experience and advising other students on dealing with the complications lying ahead in college. Soon, the work became a passion in his life that more firmly convinced him that education was a tool used not just to lift oneself up, but also to come alongside others and lift them out of their poverty-always changing something.

Entering the senior year of college, Manuel was a far cry from the uncertain teenager who questioned his place in bachelor-degree-granting higher education.

He had grown into a confident and capable young man now, ready to enter into the challenges of professional life. His journey in college had not been easy; it had been transformative. Manuel had not only gained the technical skills needed to succeed in his chosen field, but he had also developed a sense of purpose and responsibility that would guide him for the rest of his life. When Manuel graduated with a degree in electrical engineering, the moment of triumph was not his alone but belonged to the entire family. They had all sacrificed much in life to get him to this juncture, and the future was brighter than ever. Manuel was convinced that even though difficult times may still lie along the path, he was ready for all of them. His college years had given him an academic background and personal tools which will help build the life he has always aspired to. They were endless, for the first time Manuel felt completely in control of his destiny.

Chapter 6: Breaking Points and Turning Points

It was one hurdle after another in the life of Manuel Simpson, each plunging him deeper into a web of misfortunes. By age of 27, he had experienced enough hardship that would make an ordinary person throw in the towel. Quitting was never in the game for Manuel. Until then, his life had been dogged with challenges: early responsibilities, dropping out of school, young fatherhood, and a cold, harsh world that literally didn't wait for an individual to catch up. He had grown up in Indianola, Mississippi, under the care of his grandparents with daily toil in the cotton fields and carpentry-wood smell together etched in his memory.

His childhood upbringing brought him the ability to survive, but it was a rearing that gave him a certain independence in his teenage years, through which he rebelled and lost his way.

By the time, he was 17-when his wife became pregnant with his first child-Manuel thought he knew it all. He dropped out of school, trusting fully that life-with or without teachers-would teach him how to handle things. But he could not have been more wrong. Soon, he realized that without education, he was walking in the dark, confined to only lowly paid jobs and such unstable gigs that could hardly put food on the table.

The years from his late teens through mid-twenties were marked by patchwork: odd jobs here and there; one endless effort to keep body and soul together; and the growing weight of a family to provide for. He moved to Milwaukee from Illinois just looking to get away from one tough situation and landed right in the middle of another. He had three children with two different women by the time he was 20, with each relationship adding layer to layer of his life.

But the turning point came at 27, when at some fork in the road, he felt himself come to a crossroads. For years, Manuel had spiraled on a path he couldn't seem to get out of. He recalls the pains, the feeling like he was on a course he might never break free from, passing on this life of struggle onto his children. He knew that if he remained so, he would be cast into perdition.

There was a fire in him-things were not just to be left this way. He was being pushed to look into the mirror, to look at his mistakes, regrets, and fears. It was in that brutal honesty of himself that he chose the moment when enough was to be enough. He had grown tired of people telling him he couldn't, tired of feeling stuck, tired of looking at his children, knowing he wasn't setting an example they could follow.

With renewed resolve, Manuel headed back to school. It wasn't a decision taken lightly. By this time, he carried the stigma of a checkered past with mistakes that included incarceration-something society was not prone to forgive. The thought of heading back into education at an age when most people are well on their way, career-wise, was daunting. He knew he was in for a battle with personal insecurities, sitting in a class with other students who had the advantage of a clean slate.

Manuel was undeterred. He signed up for a GED program, digging into the textbooks with an eagerness he had never before experienced. This time, it wasn't about fitting into somebody else's idea of success; this was redemption-seeking, proving to his children-and perhaps most importantly, to himself-that he can be more than his past has dictated.

Every day was a challenge, but each minor triumph seemed colossal. The road wasn't smooth: Manuel's Past tried to pull him back, while whispers of doubt and judgment were everywhere he went. Some days, he thought, I must have gotten myself in just to get disappointed, that the doors I want to open will not open no matter what. But even when doubts clawed at him, he pressed on: late-night studying, poring over lessons he once would have considered beneath him. And then, slowly but surely, he began to make progress. Every page he turned, every test he passed- Building a bridge toward the future he wanted so badly.

Equally part of this journey of self-reinvention was fighting his addiction to drugs, the unseen, quiet enemy that had hidden in the shadows of his life for far too long. Drugs had been an escape, all these years, from the pain of constant failure and lost dreams. Truer to himself now, he was determined to break loose from that crutch. It was one of the most difficult things he had ever done, trying to kick the habit. It was the cravings, the temptation of falling back into that familiar numbness, and the ghostlike continuous reminders. Yet Manuel found strength in his purpose and deepened it into the image of his children, who looked up at him, waiting to see if their father truly could change.

With every relapse, with every fragile moment, he remembered why he started: a new motto to live by-if he could beat this, then he could beat anything. And with each passing day, he actually began to believe that. He learned how to replace old habits with new ones; the solace between the pages of his textbooks comforted him, while the pride he felt in himself with the slow and sure progress kept him going. The GED he earned was not just a certificate; it was a badge of how resilient he was, proof that he could do so much better than what he was unfortunately born into.

For Manuel, the process of transformation wasn't limited to education or overcoming addiction but was about shedding all the weight of his past and daring to create a future he had long ago determined was beyond him. The lessons he learned in those years were hard-earned and life-changing; he had come face-to-face with his breaking points-the moments when it felt he had no choice but to give up. But in each of those moments, he found a reason to keep going. He found a reason to believe that no matter how hard things had been, he still had the power to rewrite his story.

He looked back on his journey and knew his life had been a tapestry of failures and triumphs, mistakes and lessons learned. But what really mattered wasn't where he had been but where he was going, and he wasn't that boy anymore, one who thought the world owed him something. He was a father who knew he owed his children a better life, as a man truly understood that success is brick by brick, one decision at a time.

Manuel Simpson was finally ready to make his mark-to make peoples' lives change and understand that it is never too late to change one's path in life.

Chapter 7: Redemption Through Education and Skill Building

Manuel Simpson's route to redemption was anything but straightforward. After years of being in a vicious circle of lost opportunities, he made a beeline for doing something about it. At 27, his life stood at a crossroads, and in his depths, he knew that unless he began to take harsh measures in changing his future, he might never leave behind the ghosts of his past. This was a man who had braved the worst of life, from the stigma of imprisonment to the cruel charm of addiction and found

43

himself at the edge of a new beginning. What followed thereafter was a journey that would test his toughness, bravery, and will believe in something that he had almost forgotten existed: the possibility of a better life.

It was finishing his GED, which to someone who had dropped out of school so young felt monumental. Lining up to take the last test with strangers whose faces reflected the same anxiety he felt, Manuel couldn't shake the feeling that this test was something more than a check on his academic skills. This was a test of his willpower, a symbol of how attached he had become to himself and his children.

With every question he answered, he thought of the years he had spent in the streets, the nights sleeping under uncertainty, and the endless chain of mistakes that led him to where he could currently be found. When he finally received his score, a passing score in hand, he felt something he hadn't felt in years-pride. For the first time, he had the proof that he could do something, he could commit to a goal and see it through.

But the GED was merely a starting point. Manuel knew he had to do more to create a great, real change in his life and provide for his children more than what a high school equivalency test would ever afford him. He refused to be content, opting to further himself with certifications in various practical trades.

Odd jobs for years had exposed him to many various types of manual jobs, including carpentry and electric work. He knew skilled trades opened the way to steady, reliable income. In mastering a craft, he found himself wanting to be able to work with his hands and make something that would last-a feeling deeper than he had expected. It would be like all these skills, yielding for him not only the means to take care of his family, but serving as evidence that he had remade himself into someone capable, someone valuable.

Each new start in the different certification programs became a journey into itself. The first of his several jobs was carpentry, which somehow reminded him of his grandfather, a man he has watched build and repair with silent, consistent pride. Every time Manuel practiced the careful art of measuring and cutting, assembling, and crafting, he found a sense of connectivity to something much larger than himself.

Now, he began to realize that carpentry was a language, a way of communicating with the things he was building. He spent long hours training, learning to see the potential in rough timber, understanding even from the most modest materials, a beautiful creation could emerge through patience and skill. It was a parallel feeling to his own journey and reminded him in the same way that he, too, could shape himself into something new, something worthy.

Electrical work came next, in a field that dares him on quite different grounds. Electricity is not something to leave to chance-one mistake, one misplaced wire, could spell disaster. To think of such precision-so thrilling, so intimidating. For one who had so many years embraced chaos, learning to navigate the structured, unforgiving world of electrical systems was a revelation. Those classes were filled with men with a lot more experience-often younger men that had grown up around tools and trades. But Manuel didn't let this discourage him; he dove head-first into school, working late into the evening reviewing diagrams and notes, learning the importance of safety and the discipline of exactitude. This wasn't just about landing a job; this was an issue of self-assurance in his ability to handle responsibility-to handle something important that he could be entrusted with.

His was not a path that came with setbacks; there were times he didn't feel like doing anything, especially when his past weighed down on him like an iron shackle. People never forgot, and so he often found himself fighting the silent judgment of all those who saw him as no more than a man with a record. Even among his own, the quiet scrutiny-the unspoken questions of why he was there-palpable.

Rags 2 Riches: Lessons from the Hard Road

Employers would more often than not back away at job sites, afraid to take their chances with someone with his background. And each time he felt himself sliding back into the despair of his old life, every time that old self whispered, You will never change, he thought of his children, the legacy he wanted to leave behind. And with that thought, he plunged ahead, not to let the world define him by his mistakes.

He also learned to paint: a skill, which entailed observing the immediate impact of his work. He has never found anything quite so fulfilling as turning every drab-worn wall into one that glittered with color and life. Every stroke thus stirred the chords of his emotion: a renewal, a recall that change-whatever little this may be-is indeed possible. And as he painted, he found himself thinking of his own transformation of the layers, he was breaking away and the new ones being added.

He took pride in his work, paying attention to every little detail, savoring the knowledge that he was creating something beautiful for someone else. It was a quiet form of redemption: the way he rebuilt his reputation, one wall, one building, one satisfied client at a time.

His most challenging and unexpected certification, however, was asbestos abatement. Work was hazardous; he was entering spaces filled with hazardous material at almost any wrong move to mean exposure to something lethal. It was just that which attracted him: work that required resilience, bravery, a willingness to risk danger-a quality he has been accustomed to all his life.

Working in his protective gear, well-aware of every cautionary measure, he felt a sense of purpose that he had never had. Here was a job that was going to ask everything of him, a task that cannot be done without total dedication.

During those moments, covered head to toe in gear, carefully removing toxic materials from buildings, Manuel felt a strange sense of peace. An extremely dangerous job, but it felt almost like a calling, a glitch in the life he had long thought would be his duty to others.

Slowly but surely, Manuel got his life together, and even the lives of his children, by getting new certification after new certification, finding a step into the world of secure employment, finding work that allowed one to take care of their family. For the first time in years, he had stability in life that once seemed unreachable. He now had money put away, was renting a modest apartment and took satisfaction each day in just being able to return home from the day, knowing he had earned his own way.

The children began, for the first time, to look at him more like a father and less like the man who had fallen off the edge.

There was something different in the air as he walked, a hint of quiet strength and resolve from a journey few could understand.

Education and the building of skills became for Manuel his personal redemption, that path teaching him the value not only of hard work but also the power of transformation. He knew that, just like very few others who had been at rock bottom, his future lay in his hands. Although, the world had judged him and was quick to write him off as merely another statistic, he would not let the majority dictate his reality. For every morning, while he got dressed in his uniform, gathered his tools, he knew he told another story.

Hope was something few in Manuel's circumstances ever genuinely find. The certificates in carpentry, electrical work, painting, and asbestos abatement meant far more than mere credentials of proof of his worth, his ability to contribute, his ability to create. All these skills one by one became steppingstones, carrying him further and further away from the mistakes of his youth to the man he had always wanted to be.

Now his children had a father whom they could look up to, who had shown them that hardships in life did not need to dictate their future.

Continuing to work, Manuel began fantasizing more than he ever had. One day having his own business, hiring others in similar hard times and giving them the same chance at redemption he was given. He dreamed how his skills and story would someday inspire others, be part of a world that judged persons like him not by whom they once were but by whom they became.

Manuel Simpson had fought a hard battle, and though he was able to get his life back, his past scars remained; however, he carried them proudly, like badges of great honor. He became a living proof that change exists, it is real; redemption is alive and not a story of the mermaid far, far away, but indeed real for those who fight and struggle to achieve it. And when he looked down the path he traveled, he knew one thing for sure: his story was only just beginning.

Chapter 8: Family Dynamics and Personal Struggles

The path to stability for Manuel Simpson had his share of trials, and probably the most challenging part was treading the treacherous and mostly tumultuous relationships he had with his children's mothers. For Manuel, how to balance the fatherly duties with the demands of his new work and personal growth was a daily battle, more often overwhelming. He had changed his life in significant ways; he was certified in various trades, he had stable employment, and he had built a steady life.

As he took on the role of provider, protector, and role model for his children, he found emotionally that his life was as turbulent as ever. More than the career gains, the chemin that led to self-improvement confronted the ghosts of the past, trying to build stability and an atmosphere of love for his children amidst fragmented family dynamics.

Manuel's relationships with the mothers of his children were complicated, a reflection of mistakes he had made when he was younger. His past was riddled with choices that then seemed inconsequential but later blossomed into lifelong responsibilities. Each relationship brings its own challenges-shaped by misunderstandings, lingering resentments, and, painfully, his own history of absence. The years in prison and lost to the devil of addiction had taken their mark, no question; and while he had pulled himself out of those depths, it was still rather sensitive on an emotional level.

Gloria's mother was a woman he had met in his early twenties when neither of them was ready for responsibilities that life would shortly visit upon them. The love was short-lived and, though intense, fleeing nonetheless, which left them both with a son called Manuel JR.

Gloria was a strong woman, but her patience with Manuel had long since worn thin. She'd been there, picking up the pieces when Manuel spiralled out of control, trying to raise

Manuel JR with some semblance of normalcy while Manuel flitted in and out of his life. And now, years later, when Manuel finally got around to attempting to reach out to his son, he found that his second child named Gloria-daughter guarding him at every turn. She had seen him fail one time too many to believe this time would be any different, and while she would acknowledge the progress, he finally had made, the unspoken question always seemed to shine in her eyes: *How long will it last this time?*

Every interaction with Gloria was a reminder of lost time broken in a trust that Gloria was polite, even nice sometimes. Gloria's mother was Manuel's second wife named Jeano. However, the emotional distance in their relationship was what Manuel knew he could never truly close.

The Manuel's first childs' Mother was Liz; Michelle Jeano was my second wife and mother of my second child; Gloria Jeano was a mother of my third kid know as Manuel Jr.

Gloria wanted her father Manuel to be consistent to show up come what may Manuel JR deserved. The struggle for Manuel, though deep, was deeper: to learn to become that man, while still wrestling with a child's self-doubt. He wanted to be the stable father on whom his son could rely, but he also knew that with each misstep, he would confirm Gloria's worst fears.

Rags 2 Riches: Lessons from the Hard Road

Gloria was the mother of his second child, and she was no less problematic under the circumstances. A hot-headed woman, short-tempered, and fiercely protective of their newborn daughter, Michelle. Manuel had met when he had already begun piecing his life together but was still fighting his ghosts. Michelle had seen both sides of her father, the man who wanted to be better and the man who was still haunted by a past. They had shared a small, powerful relationship that had ended almost as soon as it began, but it was one that had left them with a deep emotional bond through their daughter.

Liz was more skeptical seeming than Jeano, but more volatile and their co-parenting relationship was often strained by her sharp criticisms and high expectations. She wanted Manuel to be present in Michelle's life, however she also wanted him to prove time and again that he was worth that privilege. Manuel knew her stand; after all, she had seen him at his worst, and she wasn't about gambling her daughter's heart on empty words.

Yet with every fight they had and every time she questioned his resolve, he couldn't help but feel that old ache of guilt and frustration. Manuel wanted to reassure her daughter Gloria of this, that the man she once knew no longer existed, but it also would not have made too much sense, as deep inside he felt he would never be able to make up for his wrongdoings in life.

These had to do with relationships; it was tricky, and he had to dig more into himself-things he was doing and the lifetime patterns he had set. Manuel often pondered his own upbringing, the things he learned from his parents and how he had failed in applying them into life. His father had been a hard, unbending man-a man who above everything else preyed on hard work and discipline. Growing up, Manuel had often felt resentful of his father's rigidity, his coldness devoid of warmth.

But now, with him being a father himself, he found himself pondering over how perhaps his dad had been right in some ways after all. What he needed for his children was discipline and consistency and he felt ironically that he was now working to become a man much like his own father but with a touch more compassion.

Meanwhile, Manuel was determined to be for his children the father he always wished he had when he was growing up-listening and present, making them feel safe and valued. It was a delicate balance, one that he wrestled to maintain, especially with the stresses of work and his ongoing personal growth. His job was physically exhausting, and some days when he came home, he was too tired to do more than collapse onto the couch. But he pushed himself-forward, knowing each moment he spent with his kids was a chance to rebuild the bond he'd so often taken for granted. He read to them, helped them with their homework, and when he could, he attended events at their school. These small acts of love and commitment had been his way of making up for lost time, his way of proving that he would be there through thick and thin.

It was perhaps a little rocky at times, but never tense. His children were still at an age in which they could remember years when papa wasn't around, and although they loved him, there was a distance in their relationship that Manuel was able to feel acutely. Manuel JR was guarded, especially, not willing to let his father fully into his life. He had grown up without a strong male figure, and Manuel's attempts to step in filled him with a mixture of curiosity and skepticism. Manuel JR was polite, even respectful, but there was a wall between them, a barrier that Manuel couldn't breach. He knew how long it would take to gain trust, that he would have to win his son's faith day by day, but it was a painful reminder of the consequences of his past.

Whereas Michelle was old enough, so more open and willing to accept her father into her life; she adored Manuel, looking up to him in a mixture of admiration and awe. She doesn't remember anything about the years she had been away to her, she was just her dad, a man who loved her and did the best he knew how. Her innocence was salve to Manuel's soul- a reminder of the hope still yet alive in him-and he treasured every second spent with her, salving every smile, every laugh, every moment of pure, unadulterated love.

Even time with Michelle had its set of difficulties. They also quarreled over decisions taken about the little one's upbringing, and sometimes Liz blamed Manuel for not being able to provide stability needed by their daughter Michelle.

Family separation complicated Manuel's efforts to become the better father, and it was a situation that weighed upon his heart as he had dreamed of a more conventional family-a life where children lived under the same roof and he could be there every day for them. It had slipped long ago, and he was left with fragments of what could have been.

His children were his world, yet they lived apart: joined onto him by threads of love and loyalty, separated by circumstances quite beyond his control. The distance that kept them asunder was a source of constant sorrow to him-a reminder of the price of his mistakes. He did his best to stay involved, to visit regularly, being present in their lives in whatever way he knew. Still, the brutal reality of being a part-time dad, sharing custody, along with complicated visitation schedules is a painful reminder of what he has to put up with.

In the process, Manuel learned and grew and further evolved. Every interaction with his children's mothers, every challenge in his relationships with his kids, taught him something new about himself and about the kind of man he wanted to become. He was determined to break this cycle, to ensure that his children would be given a better life, freed from the mistakes that haunted his own journeys. He wanted them to know, notwithstanding the flaws, how much he loved them with all his heart. He wanted them to see that redemption could be found, that people could change, and love would survive the ordeal.

But the emotional weight of his choices only made him stronger. Every struggle, every painful conversation, every moment of self-doubt was a reminder of how far he'd come and how far he still had to go. Manuel had the feeling that the path to being a better father would be very long, full of obstacles and setbacks, but he was ready to face it head-on. Because, he had run for so many years from his responsibilities, feelings, and himself, it was now time to face all three-to square up to all difficulties and to be the father his children needed.

Ultimately, Manuel's story is one of more than redemption; it is about love and resilience and the dogged belief that he can create a better future than the one he has now. The journey of healing of learning to forgive himself-to be the man he had always aspired to be. Yet, he walked the rough road with a kind of renewed purpose, feeling that with each step taken, he was closer to the family he had always wanted.

Chapter 9: Sharing His Story – Writing for Redemption

The story of Manuel Simpson is that accepting this reality and writing his story was his form of reclaiming his life and giving life to a future woven from threads of strength, determination, and love for his family. He had carried the weight of his story with him for years and had not wanted to reopen those chapters of life that has many struggles and they would pull him back down. But now he was determined to bring everything into focus to write what had been a rather up and down experience.

Since childhood, Manuel realized that no one would bring him victory; he would have to fight for it his whole life. After moving from Mississippi to Maywood Illinois, he was plunged into a culture that was wholly uninterested in him. He was no longer among those who lived in the close-knit society where people looked out for each other. Now he was in for racism in a racially segregated city, he was struggling to cope with academic demands, he was also challenged with responsibilities at home. Maywood Illinois was a world that was tough; so tough that Manuel was to make his own understandings of how he was going to cope with life, let alone making anything of it.

It is true that Manuel had a really tough time in the early years of his schooling. At Emerson School, he was new, the guy with a different accent and coming from South. His fellow students saw him as a stranger, and his teachers appeared to lose their patience with him, and did not assist him to overcome the challenges that were put to him academically. Still, despair was not an option for Manuel, so he did not let that seed grow inside of him. He worked in school after classes, re-did his lessons and made an effort to be the best he can be. These years, he would later come to discover were actually preparing him for the next phase.

Rags 2 Riches: Lessons from the Hard Road

His story continued writing and as he did so he recalled how he realized that it was difficult to be a father and at the same time try to rebuild his life. Every one of his children had a special position in his affection, but the paternity did not bring happiness to his relationships with the children's mothers. His first child was Michelle whom he had when he was young and working on his dreams, the second child was Gloria, whom he had to have while struggling to carve an existence for himself. His son, Manuel Jr., added a new dimension to the story; here was a young boy whose father needed him, but Manuel was strained with Jeano, Gloria's mother.

Every meeting with his children's mothers was a kind of personal victory and a lesson of something in him as a man, in him as a failure, in him as a success. Some of these were tough and he was left with certain guilt feelings and self-concerns. Yet, he wrote, willing to record such moments as they are. To Manuel, there was some form of catharsis in owning up for our mistakes, accepting the consequences of his decisions and most important, choosing to let those past errors shape or determine the rest of his life.

Redemption he saw was not one as he thought but a process and a process that was repeated in several steps. He had indeed traveled a notch higher from just holding temporary jobs and at times even low self-esteem. He had gone through the hustle of getting certification, getting a decent job, and establishing himself. As little things as learning how to paint were always liberating and something that was very concrete, which gave him an opportunity to constantly express himself. Every wall he painted was new, a new canvas he was giving a new chance to make something beautiful for other people.

Manuel was as much a triumph of narrative as it was a case study about how not to go through life; but to learn from one's mistakes and to fight against one's society's prejudices. When he began to write, he wanted people who might be suffering to hear this story from him telling them that anything is possible even in the worst of times. People could always be given hope and when Manuel was writing, he could share all that he had learnt and wanted others to know that they too could change if they tried.

For Manuel writing was also associated with misery memories that he had faced the worst situation of his life, when he was an addict of drugs and used to ruin his life completely. Analyzing, he had been 27 years by the time, and he understood that if he did not turn his life around, he will be stuck with the path of lost chances. He had witnessed many of his peers die in similar ways, individuals who just lost all their hope, their money, and their jobs. Of course, Manuel could not let things get that way, he had a goal to better his life regardless of the moments of indecision crossed his mind.

Some days, he came very close to quitting to throwing in the towel on his education, his job, and the dream of something better. Each time he realized that he still has a way of continuing. He considered his family, his children and the man that he wanted to be and that they should see him as father. To this, writing enabled him to make the necessary reflections on these moments, make the right conclusions regarding the need for perseverance, to do so and never say never when it comes to himself.

Manuel's life is about learning and living with new purpose through the sharing of his experience, and that purpose transcends his own experience. He wrote with the intention of making the voices of those who felt unheard and informing those who thought the path was too difficult. He had been there, done that, or something to that effect; he had been there and come out the other end. And now, with this story, he offered people a look at that journey, every time he took one step forward, he could be forgiven and could find redemption with a true path of success.

Chapter 10: Reflections and Lessons Learned

Even writing was tough for Manuel as it uncomfortably vividly recalled the worst moments he had to face–days of addiction as well as the resulting mistakes he made.

Each time he realized that he still has a way of continuing learning throughout his life prospects. He considered his family, his children and the man that he wanted to be and that they should see him as a role model. It created an opportunity to write and think how such moments were valuable for as a lesson in hard work and never giving up.

Rags 2 Riches: Lessons from the Hard Road

Others still seen writing as a way to bring back memories that came along with moments that he admitted he thought he wouldn't have the chance to live again. It characterizes Manuel who didn't want to end up in the terrible situations; he still dreamt of a better life despite the moments' self-recognition.

From family background, Manuel realized how important it was to be a first–generation college student. His parents were from the Deep South, and they were barely literate; they worked hard to support their family. And yes, that was just the end goal, not just his triumph, but the triumph of his family as well. It symbolized freedom from the traditions set by previous generations of proving that with determination and perseverance as well as not taking 'no' for an answer success can be achieved where failure had always reigned. It provided him with a sense of pride and with something to do. He summed it up to understand that after all, it was not just about himself as well as those who preceded him and those that would succeed him. He made it his life's work to make his children and other people dream despite the circumstances in their lives.

Manuel's thinking also led him to an important insight regarding choice. He had not had a plain sailing and agreed with some of the difficulties being as a consequence of choices that he had made. He had made decisions that have distorted rapport between him and others and also brought personal misfortunes. But instead of being held back by regret and remorse, he was able to take these experiences as lessons. The weaknesses that he committed had shaped him on matters to do with integrity, honesty, and self-discipline. He realized for the first time that this was the price for growth, responsibility and he vowed to be a better man.

Besides the work experiences, during his looking back, Manuel also identified values such as community and friendship. During his playschool and later, in school and college, he found friends to lean on, friends who encouraged him. He met with people that were going through the same experiences as him, and together they engaged in measures that made the journey little bearable. It was a nice reminder to have these relationships to show him that everyone has their own problems to deal with. He understood that it is alright, in fact good to rely on other people when they can support him in times of weakness and he applied this aspects too to the others aspects of life.

Lastly, Manuel's reflections brought him to one of his most important realizations: the power of hope. Whereas, in the hopelessness and confusion that had seemed to engulf him at times, hope had been his beacon. For a better future he had to endure all what he had as a childhood, his education, and his relationships with his children. It was the one thing that had been able to sustain him each time all odds were against him. He learned hope is about a feeling that becomes a will to believe in the abstract of change and progress.

This story of Manuel was not only an end for him but a recapitulation of the knowledge he had accumulated on his odyssey. Every lesson, each reflection that had been taught and shared within the classroom each day had helped mold him for the man that he has become and the father he dreams to be. His story was a story of struggling and rising again, it instilled some deep spirit that no matter how pathetic your past is; there is always room to turn for better if only you will work for it.